About the Authors:

Fred Warren is a professor of music at Sonoma State College in Northern California, coordinator of African studies at the University of California extension at Santa Cruz, and has served as both coordinator and lecturer in African music programs at the Berkeley campus as well.

In 1968, Dr. Warren received a U.S. State Department grant which sent him to Africa to collect materials on African culture for use in schools; at the same time, his wife Lee was acting as Official Escort to the Ghana Dance Ensemble on its state-wide tour of University of California campuses. Together, Dr. and Mrs. Warren traveled to Algiers for the first Pan-African Cultural Festival in 1969.

Dr. Warren has written a number of magazine and newspaper articles on African music, and has recently finished work on an African songbook.

DATE DUE

DATE DUE			
FEB 2 8			
MAR 1			
MAY 0 2 1994			

ILLUSTRATED WITH PHOTOS AND
LINE DRAWINGS BY PENELOPE NAYLOR

THE MUSIC

OF

AFRICA

AN INTRODUCTION

BY

DR. FRED WARREN

WITH

LEE WARREN

PRENTICE-HALL, INC., ENGLEWOOD CLIFFS, N.J.

Designed by Leslie Bailey

Library of Congress Catalog Card Number: 73-125329
Printed in the United States of America • J
ISBN-0-13-608224-6

Prentice-Hall International, Inc., London
Prentice-Hall of Australia, Pty. Ltd., Sydney
Prentice-Hall of Canada, Ltd., Toronto
Prentice-Hall of India Private Ltd., New Delhi
Prentice-Hall of Japan, Inc., Tokyo

CONTENTS

FOREWORD

Little notice was taken of African music until the middle of the 19th century. Why was it ignored for so long? Part of the answer can be found in the extremely narrow concept of the word "music" held by Europeans and Americans. Music was considered to be a melody one could sing or whistle, or a masterwork composed by a Mozart or a Beethoven performed on the piano, violin or clarinet or other instruments of the orchestra. Measured by these criteria, Africans have been making only noise, not music. There are no African Mozarts or Beethovens, and African instruments are unlike anything we see in our orchestras.

Some of the explanation is also rooted in the 19th century evangelical drive into Africa by Christian missionaries. All music which was not morally and spiritually uplifting according to Christian standards was either discouraged or prohibited. This only served to increase the ignorance and misconceptions about African music.

But the most significant reason for the Western world's non-acceptance of Africa's music is to be found in the attitudes of Europeans and Americans toward Black Africans. There is often a correlation between one's feelings about people and one's attitude toward the music they make. Africans had been colonized, exploited and enslaved by Europeans and Americans for hundreds of years. It is virtually impossible for one group of people to inflict terrible damage on another group without regarding them as inferior members of the human race. Differences between peoples and cultures become inequalities under such conditions. If Africans are inferior and uncivilized, then so must be their music. Therefore why pay serious attention to a music which was inferior, primitive and crude?

This is the backdrop for the musical culture of a gigantic land mass — a land mass that is as unique in both size and exotic qualities as it is for the accumulation of myths and fallacies that exist about its people and history. It may seem strange, or even presumptuous to undertake to write about the music of Africa as if it were a small and culturally homogenized area. If Africa is, in fact, a vast continent with many different nations and many different ethnic groups, each having its own traditions and language, how can we write about African music as if Africa were *one* country or one tribe rather than *many*?

We do it in the same spirit with which our space explorers examine the distant and mysterious terrestrial bodies. We first became familiar with the moon from an immense distance. From this vantage point we made certain generalizations about its form and shape, its climatic conditions, the nature of its surface, and so on. Scientists, however, never stop in their investigation of highly specialized aspects of the moon.

We will look at the music of Africa from the same perspective of explorers approaching a hitherto undiscovered subject. And it is our hope that this introduction to African music as a whole will stimulate the reader to further examine the many different kinds of music produced by the many different peoples of Africa.

THE PLACE OF MUSIC
IN TRADITIONAL
AFRICAN LIFE

Africa is huge. Her size is more than three times that of the United States. Her visual splendors are a feast of endless variety, horizon-touched grasslands, snow-capped mountains, rain forests, jungles and deserts. The rich, bright colors of the people's everyday clothes and ceremonial garments and the Noah's Ark of animals and birds weave together a magnificent scene.

But the sounds of Africa are the most wonder-filled things of all. It is a continent where at least eight hundred languages are spoken. If you could travel from Senegal to Sudan, from Togo to Tanzania, you would hear languages you never dreamed existed. Even in a small country such as Ghana in West Africa you can hear different languages, depending on which part of the country you are in. It is not at all uncommon for the people of one tribe to be unable to understand the people of another tribe living only a few miles away. And across this vast continent, across its fifty different countries inhabited by two hundred fifty million people, your ear is captured by the thrilling sounds of African music.

Just as Africa has been a dark mystery to most of us, much is unknown about the music and the people who make it. Mention "African music" and the image usually conjured up is one of Africans beating on drums and making strange and awful sounds. Forty or fifty years ago, few people were prepared to pay serious attention to the music of Africa. It was usually dismissed as savage and primitive, unworthy of either scholarly or listening attention, not to mention performance. As one country after another achieved its independence, the old colonial regimes were forced out and new concepts of what Africa and Africans are like were thrust upon the Western world. Ranking high among the most important and exciting aspects of African culture, music is an essential part of every facet of daily life.

The Africa we will discuss is south of the Sahara, or Black Africa. The music of north Africa is quite distinct from the music of the rest of the continent and is generally classified as Arabic music. Although this land to the south is inhabited by numerous ethnic groups, each having its own musical tradition, there are certain musical characteristics which many of them share.

For many people, the words "primitive" or "uncivilized" would be the description automatically applied to African music and to its source, the African, since music and its maker cannot be separated. But up until a short time ago, many uninformed people regarded jazz, a product of the black man's experience in America, as a primitive or uncivilized kind of music. It is no accident or coincidence that until recently the black man's music, both jazz and African, has been ignored. Even today when a student enrolls in a course entitled "Music Appreciation" or "History of

Music" he is not likely to be introduced to the music which has been a part of the lives of millions of Africans.

Unfortunately, too many of us have thought of the European as being the only truly civilized member of the human race and possessor of the only music worthy of study, appreciation and performance. From the moment we enter school, we are taught to appreciate *this* music as opposed to the "primitive" or "inferior" music of the non-European world. When we become adult members of our highly civilized society we attend concerts and operas and passively ingest music like vitamins that are good for us.

In our Western civilization, music performs a variety of functions. Most of these functions, however, are not vital to our existence. Music can entertain us after a hard day's work; it can take our minds away from everyday cares and troubles; it can, at times, provide us with a deeply moving emotional experience. But the point is that we can carry on the important activities of day-to-day living without music. This is unthinkable in traditional African societies.

For the African, music is not a luxury, but a part of the process of living itself. Although Africa is inhabited by peoples who represent many different life styles, the one common denominator for all Africans is their love of music and their almost total involvement with it. Music follows the African through his entire day from early in the morning till late at night, and through all the changes of his life, from the time he came into this world until after he has left it.

When we talk about music in the African way of life, let us make no mistake about what we mean when we say that music is an integral part of a life style. For all the plateaus reached in the journey from birth to puberty, for example, there are traditional songs and dances that are completely necessary to the rituals celebrating each milestone. In our society, a baby can be born, taken home from the hospital, assume his place as a member of the family unit, and receive appropriate gifts from his uncles, cousins and aunts, without a single musical sound being made, apart from, perhaps, the baby's crying.

In an African village, the musical tradition surrounding the birth of a child begins before the baby is born. It is the witch doctor whom the young woman approaches in order to be assured that she will have a successful delivery. The witch doctor sings and dances to make sure that all will go well. Afterward the family, or possibly even the entire village, will join in the singing of a special song for the occasion.

There is special music for the ceremony celebrating the birth of the baby and, if twins are born, the villagers (especially the women) outdo themselves with their dancing and singing. The naming of the baby and the appearance of its first tooth are both honored in song and dance. A child in Dahomey is taught a song which he sings on the loss of his first tooth. The Akan people of Ghana have a special song for the habitual bed wetter, sung by other children at a special ritual, designed to shame the bed wetter into drier behavior.

Reaching the age of puberty is a momentous occasion. Songs make up part of the circumcision rites for boys and among some Africans, boys are taught various songs in the evening while waiting for their wounds to heal.

In our society, intelligent and thoughtful parents will often give their child a special book which explains the "facts of life"; fathers have talks with their sons and mothers

4

*NOTCHED FLUTES

*An asterisk preceding a caption indicates
that details may be found in the Appendix.

share their wisdom with their daughters. In African societies, it is through the traditional songs and dances that young men and women receive their instruction in family living and learn about the customs and practices, the obligations and responsibilities which are part of growing up and assuming one's place in the adult community.

When girls reach puberty, they are taught what a grown woman must do. The music and dancing which is performed at the ceremony are designed to help the girl learn how to become a woman and a mother, and serve as a crash course on the customs and history of her tribe as well. Among certain peoples in Ghana, the girls go around the town performing the puberty dance for several days after the completion of the puberty ritual, and collect gifts from onlookers. Instruction, quite naturally, includes the manner in which the marriage rites will be performed. All this vital know-how is communicated through actions, dance, and most especially, through song.

The flow of life continues its time-honored, predictable way. Boy meets girl, boy marries girl. The singing and dancing at marriage ceremonies go on for hours with hundreds of people participating.

At other times songs are sung in honor of loved ones who have died. After burial, sad songs become more joyful, in an effort to help the relatives of the deceased turn their minds away from the death. This last performance is kept as happy as possible. (The high-stepping brass band of America's South, joyously marching with the parade of mourners to the tune of "When the Saints Go Marching In," is a true descendant of this tradition.)

Many songs closely follow the seasons and the traditional yearly events. There are songs at the new moon, songs at various agricultural festivals. There is hardly a month in which a festival of some sort is not celebrated in some locality. These festivals and the music which has become an inseparable part of them play an important role in giving Africans the feeling of kinship and loyalty in their community. They can, to some degree, be compared with our American small town or county fairs. Again, while all kinds of music will be going on at the fair to entertain people and give the event a holiday atmosphere, there are certain required songs and dances that must be performed at the African festivals which would simply not be complete without them.

There are songs to persuade the spirits into benevolence before some project is undertaken, songs to bring rain, and songs chanted for protection against fire and danger. "Music for all occasions" could very well be the carrying card of the African.

Warrior organizations have their own music, although not all their music and dances are warlike. Traditionally, of course, music was as much a part of battle as the weapons in the hands of the fighting men.

There's an interesting story told of a battle between the British and the Ashanti in the early part of the nineteenth century. The British were the colonial rulers at that time and they brought with them into battle a military band of African musicians. During the fighting, a British general heard the sounds of the royal trumpet music coming out of the Ashanti camp. He responded by having his musicians play the British National Anthem, to show the Ashanti that their opposition had the full weight of the British Empire behind them. But the Ashanti, unaware that they were supposed to be cowed by this evidence of British invulnera-

APENTEMMA DRUM, PLAYED WITH PALMS OF HAND
OR FINGERS

bility, placed a different interpretation on the music, went on the offensive, defeated the Royal African Corps and captured the British general.

Changing times create new functions for traditional music. For instance, Asafo, the music of warrior organizations, has become a feature of political rallies in modern-day Ghana. In peacetime, warrior organizations function as associations with their own rituals, ceremonies and festivals. As a matter of fact, during peacetime, they may be responsible for clearing paths, building bridges and organizing search parties.

The ongoing struggle for independence is reflected in songs of protest. Even on a more personal level, the scolding of an individual for misbehavior will often be contained in a song. For example, a woman who has been eyeing another woman's husband will be publicly chastised in the marketplace. The other women of the village will rebuke her and shame her in song, a polite way of putting the flirt back on the road of virtue.

Naturally, there are songs of love and there is also music with no more serious purpose than to relax with for a couple of hours—blowing on a flute or plunking on a thumb piano. The fact that much of African music is integrated with other activities, both social and political, does not mean that an African will not make music privately for his own amusement. The sight of the lonely traveler playing his thumb piano as he meanders along is not an uncommon one in some parts of Africa.

In many African societies there are songs which are part of the ceremonies conducted to heal the sick. The spells and prayers of medicine men which are accompanied by

MBIRA — THUMB PIANO

singing and dancing often do produce healing. Modern
psychiatrists who recently did research in Africa believe
that the hypnotic suggestions of the witch doctor and the
frantic possession dances are really ancient methods of
curing mental illnesses.

Memorable events, from the election of a village chief to
the capture of an elephant, are celebrated in song. In the
court music of the Banum people of Cameroon there is
even an impressive and eerie piece to be used on the occasion of the hanging of a government minister.

While we in America do not have any particular music
to relate to the capture of an elephant or the hanging of a
cabinet member, we do have ceremonies in which music

*HAND RATTLE

plays an essential role. One example among many is the performance of "Hail to the Chief" as an integral part of the inauguration of the President of the United States.

Some African music is explicitly functional. That is, there are times when an African will employ the sounds of music in order to get a job done. For example, a number of people, including the Fali of North Cameroon, eat termites. (If you think this is exceedingly unusual behavior in view of the fact that most Western societies hire exterminators to kill termites, remember that the French regard the snail as a delicacy, to the amazement of those who take great pains to destroy them in their gardens.) They have developed a method of drumming (the Fali tap with sticks on upturned calabashes) so that the termites down below think it is raining and come popping up to the surface.

Children absorb much of their basic knowledge by imitating their elders. It cannot be overemphasized that in traditional African societies, children are not taught by books. They are not even taught verbally. Virtually all instruction takes place through actions, dances and, especially, songs. "Follow the leader" in song is an African specialty and the innumerable game songs the grownups teach the little ones establish a solid foundation for all areas of learning. Children learn to count by song. They learn the language of their tribe in song.

The African child learns about life through music. His mother sings to him throughout childhood, even when he is a tiny baby. Through songs he learns about the members of his family and the important people, places and events of his community, his tribe and his country. By singing songs which contain a moral, his mother teaches him what his people consider to be right or wrong.

Songs can serve a dual purpose. A lullaby used to calm a child into sleep may also contain reflections of the singer's own feelings. It may even include a message to the husband who is paying too much attention to another woman:

> *"Bonnie bouncy crybaby,*
> *Come for a feed.*
> *If you divorce me,*
> *You cannot take my child.*
> *Bonnie bouncy crybaby,*
> *Come for a feed."*

The mother whose wifely status is threatened by a rival and the possibility of a divorce, rocks her baby to a cradle song, which serves both to reassure herself and to remind the wandering husband that in the matrilineal society of the Akan people of Ghana a child belongs to the mother's lineage:

"Someone would like to have you for her child,
But you are my own.
Someone wished she had you to nurse you
*   on a good mat,*
Someone wished you were hers.
She would put you on a camel blanket,
But I have you, to rear you on a torn mat.
Someone wished she had you,
But I have you."

Music also plays an essential role in the political life of African society. It is through music that people learn about their political institutions and the laws of their community; in the same way—through music—they express their feelings about politics and politicians. This is a natural consequence for a society in which all kinds of information is passed along by means of songs, dances and storytelling, rather than written down in books. We must realize, of course, that in traditional African societies music making is not the exclusive domain of the musician. Everyone makes up songs and frequently they are spontaneous and topical. The texts of these songs are often specifically political and present evaluation and judgment of public policy and public officials.

*FONTOMFROM ENSEMBLE

In some traditional West African societies, there were people who specialized in the craft of political music making. They were known as Griots and they imparted a variety of political information throughout the community. In a real sense, the Griot did what most Africans in traditional societies did, only much better. He was a professional who specialized in words, spoken and sung. He might have been a tanner, a blacksmith or a weaver. His craft, however, was music.

The Griot was also a narrator of history. He made the past come to life. As one African has said, "Other people use writing to record the past, but they no longer *feel* the past because writing does not have the warmth of the human voice."

In present-day, independent Mali, the musician informs his audience of the policies of the government. He sings of African unity and of the Five-Year Plan. He sings the praises of specific governmental projects such as a new factory and of different groups of workers. In Ghana, which has been ruled by a military tribunal since 1966, criticism of the government can be found in songs sung by professional musicians. Music also plays a vital role in the black African's struggle for freedom in parts of southern Africa today.

The praise song was, and is, common all over Africa, as eulogy to a chief or other dignitary, and in these days, often to a president or prime minister. Such songs arouse feelings of loyalty in the listener. In America it is customary to honor a prominent person, such as an astronaut, a baseball player, or a senator, by making a speech. It is less common to laud him in music. Imagine a graduating class being honored in song rather than by a commencement speech!

Such noble homage still occurs in Africa and seems to be evenly distributed over the greater part of the continent.

Fallen idols no longer receive praise songs in their honor. Songs which praised Kwame Nkrumah,* the former Ghanaian president, are no longer to be found on the "top forty" praise song charts.

By now it is an understatement to say that for the African, music and life are one. What, where and how a song is sung is a matter of time-honored procedure. On the other hand, there are occasions when tradition demands the *absence* of music. With the Ashanti, for example, singing or whistling while bathing is discouraged. This is due to the superstition that it might cause the death of a relative. In the capital of Akwapim (one of the Akan states) whistling at night is prohibited.

African music should not be judged in Western terms as being "good" music but in African terms as being "good for what purpose?" "What is the function of the music?" "What is it intended to do?" "Is it successful at doing it?" For example, a plowing song is said to have the power to make the crops grow. The specific song for plowing must be used correctly, or the harvest will suffer.

If you can imagine the students of one of our Ivy League schools participating in special songs and dances before the "big" game, to help their team win that game, and that the team's victory or defeat depends on how well the music and dance was performed, you can begin to get an idea of the role that music plays in the life of the African.

Religion plays an important role in traditional African thought, weaving together the sacred and the secular. In

* Nkrumah was overthrown by a military coup in February, 1966 and is at present living in exile in Guinea.

*MUSICAL BOW, PLAYED LIKE A JEW'S HARP

many times and places, music has been identified with creation, birth, death and rebirth. The Orphic legends present just one example. The Dogon of Mali believe that music, and more precisely, the drum, was the vehicle through which the Word of God was brought to man. In a sense, then, without music to bestow the blessing, human activity is bound to fail. Given this attitude, we can see that much of African music is not really meant to be heard by humans. It is meant to be *sung* by them. What is vital is that if the music is performed well, the crops will grow.

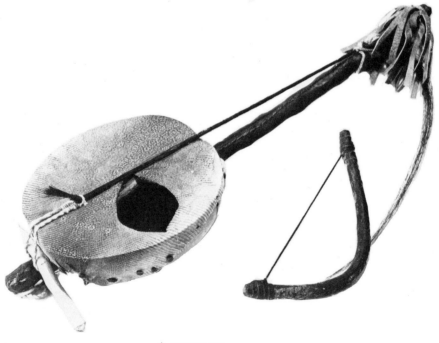

* GONDJE

There are almost no words capable of describing the intensity of the African's need for music. A suggestion of this profound attachment to music is revealed in statements made to the famous American anthropologist, Alan Merriam, when he visited the Basongye people in the Republic of the Congo (Leopoldville). The feeling expressed was, "If there were no musicians in this village, I would move someplace else where there *are* musicians." These words came from people who greatly value and depend on family relationships and have equally strong feelings about traditional land ownership. When you realize that they would be willing to leave a native village for musical reasons, you begin to get a glimmer of the life-supporting need of music to the African.

Over eighty percent of all people living south of the Sahara live in the country, not in towns or industrial areas. And the music we're speaking of is the traditional music which permeates the African villages. The traditional or folk music of Africa, associated with the traditional African institutions of the pre-colonial era, has survived in these villages and withstood the impact of foreigners. One way in which this was accomplished was when an African left the village to live in the city, he got together with other immigrants and formed immigrant clubs in which they continued to practice their traditional music and dances. Nigerian dance clubs are found in Ghana, just as Ghanaian dance clubs are found in the capitals of Liberia and Mali.

The popular or dance music heard in the cities of Africa today presents no problem to a Westerner. African pop music, known as *Highlife*, sounds very much like traditional American jazz, with strong emphasis on Afro-Cuban rhythms. The instruments used are familiar: trumpets, saxophones and guitars. Soul music is enjoyed in all the larger cities of Africa and Aretha Franklin, James Brown and Otis Redding are household names to the young Africans there. However, even these young moderns, who constitute a minority of the African population, remember the music of their parents and grandparents, and the role which music played, and continues to play, in the lives of the millions of Africans still in the villages.

Wherever the music is—in the country and in the cities—the performers and audiences alike are magnificently unrestrained. Africans are outgoing and dramatic in their behavior when they make music. Performers move their bodies in total rapport with the music and the audience wails and howls as an expression of appreciation and encouragement.

It is only natural that the African's attitude toward music will be affected by the kind of functional role it plays. We find it quite normal to talk about the beauty of a melody and to describe it as being "pleasant." But not so the African; he uses the word "pleasing" instead of "pleasant." We think of a piece of music as being beautiful in its own right. The African describes a melody in terms of what it does for an individual or his community.

We give music an independent life of its own. When a melody is created or a song is composed, it is written down. It is then given a title, the composer's name is attaced to it, it is copyrighted and it becomes an object to be sold for profit. For the African, the entire process of producing music has been a matter of creating it, performing it, and sharing it—having it heard and remembered and performed, in turn, by others. In a real sense it resembles our jazz music during its early days when its creators played it, and did not find it necessary to write it down.

To the African, music is not an independent thing or object but rather, a means to an end. It is part of the *way* of doing something. The African boatman sings as he paddles. Herdboys play flutes as they watch the cattle. Soldiers sing to set a rhythm for their marching. Music is part of the action, as natural as breathing.

For us, music is an expression of art. We have professional composers, musicians and performers whose job it is to entertain us and to enrich our lives. The difference in Africa is that music making is not confined to the professional. It is the concern of everyone. It is uncommon for

*KALUNGU

the African to play *for* someone. He would rather play *with* someone. The solo singer draws a spontaneous reaction of singing, handclapping, and dancing from those who stand nearby. Everyone takes part in what is going on.

It is in music and dance that the African is most himself. If we are to understand him as a human being, we must try to understand his music. To do this, it is necessary to know how African music is put together as well as the role that it plays in his everyday life. Singular and special to the African, it is different in structure and in sound from ours.

Certainly, it is difficult to describe music verbally. The attempt to reconstruct one art form with the tools of another must, inevitably, be less than perfect. However, the exploration of African music in words will have its frustration lessened with the reward of the exciting discovery of the African's world, where music and the African are, after all, one.

DOUBLE GONG —
SOMETIMES USED AS
"TALKING" INSTRUMENT

MELODY IN
AFRICAN MUSIC

Ours is best! There is that familiar certainty of superiority in the unfortunate but commonplace assumption that our own music, the music of Western civilization, is the only true music, the only music, in fact, which makes any sense. Not surprisingly, therefore, most people start out with the suspicion that African music is incomprehensible and upon first listening to it, are convinced their initial hunch was correct.

Since the African melodies we hear are full of intervals which to our Western ears are either too long or too short, it is little wonder that we question whether the African can manage to carry a tune, let alone create one.

Some basic definitions are a necessary first step in understanding any music:

(1) An *interval* in music is the distance between two tones or pitch levels.

(2) A *melody* consists of a series of intervals (and, for most of us, not just any old series of intervals but one which "makes sense"—that is, a series of intervals which we can whistle or sing or hum).

(3) A *scale* is a particular pattern of intervals. You might think of it in terms of a ladder where there is a specific distance between each rung (interval) and the ladder itself is the scale. You can easily prove to yourself how much we have become accustomed to a particular kind of scale made up of specific intervals which give rise to a certain type of melody. If you were asked to sing a scale consisting of eight different tones, calling the first one "Do," and then proceeding upwards, calling the next one "Re," the third one "Mi" and so on through "Fa," "So," "La," "Ti" and, once again, "Do," the odds are highly in favor that even without the benefit of a musical education you would sing the same scale, or pattern of intervals. In other words, you would produce the same musical ladder. To make the point clearer yet, if numbers one through eight are substituted for Do, Re, Mi, etc., and if you were asked to sing the following melody, consisting of the following intervals,

1	2	3	1
1	2	3	1
3	4	5	
3	4	5	

chances are that within a brief period of time you would find yourself singing the first part of the French folk song, "Frere Jacques." This could only happen because we have been brought up in a culture whose music has been based to such an extraordinarily large degree on the Major scale, the pattern of intervals which was so comfortable for you when you sang "Do," "Re," "Mi" or one through eight.

One of the reasons why African melodies are confusing to us is that they don't seem to fit into our Western scales. It comes down to this: The problem we have in listening to African music is really based on our listening point of view.

We regard the Major scale and the melodies based on it as natural, right, correct, hum-able, singable. The minute we get into a culture whose melodies consist of intervals which are larger and smaller than ours and which do not acknowledge our scale structure, then we have melodies which are strange to our ears. Sometimes we even deny that these are melodies at all, simply because they are not the same singable, hum-able, whistle-able type of tunes with which we are familiar.

If an African were asked to sing our Major scale (re- member the "Do," "Re," "Mi," "Fa," "So," "La," "Ti," "Do"?), he wouldn't know how unless, of course, he had been educated in a European or American school, learning to make music "correctly," as we do.

The Westerner has divided the octave (the distance between the first and eighth notes of the Major scale), into twelve equally distanced steps. When all twelve notes within an octave are played or sung, we are creating what is known as a chromatic scale. The overwhelming majority of the music with which we are familiar, however, is based upon the "Do-Re-Mi" scale which consists of seven out of the twelve notes within the octave.

Many Africans also use a seven-step scale.* However, the distance between their scale intervals are not exactly the same as ours. It is only because we have not been able

* Others use six-interval scales and still others use five-interval scales.

to devise symbols which will enable us to accurately transcribe an African melody, that is, to write it down on paper exactly as it is sung by an African, that we use our Western scales as a basis for writing African music. It should not, however, be assumed, as it is so often, that the Western scale is superior to all others.

As far as the African is concerned, scales as we know them do not even exist. He does not think in terms of scales or keys and is, therefore, much freer than we are in the composition of his music. We must remember that no matter how hard we try, it is virtually impossible to talk about African music in *our* musical terms. The concept of the scale, whether it be a five-note scale, a six-note scale or a seven-note scale, with precise intervals between each step of the scale, is within *our* frame of musical reference, and not within *his*.

It is similar to attempting to talk about the kinds of melodies which were created and performed by the first-generation jazz musician who, without benefit of a formal music education, produced sounds which we could not put down on paper, which we could not reproduce on the piano because, somehow, the notes seemed to slip into the cracks between the keys—the birth of the "blue" notes. They were the sound of jazz and represented the Afro-American's inability to cope with European melodies and scales.

The problem of transcribing African music into our music language is nearly impossible to solve and will remain impossible until we develop a music language which can deal with African music on its terms and not on ours.

By forcing African music into our scale patterns, for example, we are, in a real sense, distorting the music.

African melodies are formed and shaped to a large degree by the words with which they are associated. Much of African music is connected with some kind of text. And song text plays a markedly more important role in the composition of an African song than is the case with American or European songs because most African languages are tonal languages. The words have their own melodic lines—that is, some words are spoken in a high-pitched voice, some in a low-pitched voice and others somewhere in the middle. It is the melodic line or varying pitch levels which make the words understandable in the first place. Unlike songs in English, African melodies normally follow the melodic line of the text. For example, in the language called Twi (the mother tongue of about three million Ghanaians) a word can have more than one meaning, depending upon whether it is spoken in a high-pitched voice or a low-pitched voice. Take the word *Kɔkɔ*. It means "chest" when the second syllable is high pitched—Kokɔ́. The same word—Kɔ́kɔ—means "hill" when the first syllable is high pitched and the second is low pitched. The phrase, *Kyére sé* means "unless" and the same phrase, with different pitch emphasis—*Kyeré se*—means "so that."

These are the vowels in Twi with their English equivalents:

U as the *oo* sound in boot
First sound of
O as the *uo* sound in quote

27

Second sound of
o as the *u* sound in put

ɔ as the *O* sound in dot
a as the *a* sound in at
e as the *e* sound in pet
First sound of
e as the *ea* sound in great
Second sound of
e as the *e* sound in reply
i as the *i* sound in machine.

Because of the melodic contour of words in African tonal languages, a performer will very often follow the rise and fall of the text so closely that the non-African listener can sometimes find it difficult to decide whether he is listening to speaking or singing. In African music the words and melody are inseparable. It is important to understand that there is not a slavish, unchanging pattern in the relationship between words and melody line. The combination is flexible, easily accommodating to the will and mood of the performer.

Improvisation, the art of spontaneous creation of both words and melody, is a highly regarded skill and those singers who are particularly accomplished in this field enjoy great public acclaim.

The song-like quality of African words and phrases helps to explain why, with the exception of the Swahili language on the east coast of Tanzania and Kenya, there is almost no rhymed poetry to be found in all of Africa. Instead one finds blank verse with beautiful phrasing and it is the phrasing that takes the place of rhyme. Since the tonal nature of African languages requires that special attention be paid to the rise and fall of pitch, the step from a spoken phrase to a sung stanza is small and may explain why Africans find it so easy and natural to sing.

When Africans get together to sing they are not concerned that some of the group sing the melody and others provide the harmony. Quite often Africans sing their melodies in unison, that is, everyone sings at the same pitch level. Or, the men and women may sing the same notes an octave apart. A striking characteristic of African music is the *organum* principle, sometimes called *parallelism* whereby a second part is added to the main melody. But, unlike our music, the second part is not a supporting melody which "harmonizes" with the main melody, it is *exactly* the same melody, only sung parallel to it, the distance or interval of a fourth or a fifth below, that is, four or five scale steps below. The effect can be truly magnificent.

The absence of a written African musical language, with scales and keys, melody and harmony, supposedly allows the African to enjoy a freedom which the Western musician has long been working toward. "Primitive" is as outdated an image of African music as it is of the Africans themselves. Which is more primitive, music which generally proceeds in one of two kinds of scale patterns or keys (Major and Minor) or music which makes constant use of a great variety of "scales" and "keys"? (Remember, in Western music, keys are of two kinds—*Major* and *Minor*—according to whether they are based on the notes of the Major or Minor scale. In *all* Major or Minor keys, the relationship between the notes of the scale are *exactly the same*.) Which is more primitive, music which has two scales with fixed intervals or that which has a large number of "scales" with varying intervals? Who is more "primitive," the performer who must always be dependent on written melodies or the one who can improvise freely?

A significant comparison could be made between the African's way of creating his music and our present-day avant-garde composers. Modern artists in our culture are struggling to break away from conventional Western musical concepts. They could learn a great deal from the African and his music.

AFRICAN DRUMSTICK

30

RHYTHM IN
AFRICAN MUSIC

R hythm in African music has always been an object
of fascination for Westerners. It is certainly one of its most
outstanding aspects. The rhythmic style is commonly referred to as *polyrhythm*. Polyrhythm is two or more basic
rhythmic patterns going on at the same time. For example,
imagine two people clapping a "marching" rhythm and a
"waltz" rhythm simultaneously. That is, one person claps
the rhythmic pattern, **1** 2/ **1** 2/ etc., and, *at the
same time*, the other claps the rhythmic pattern **1** 2 3/
etc. This is an "uncomplicated" example of how the African approaches rhythm.

Visitors to Africa are immediately, inevitably impressed
by their remarkable sense of rhythm. We remember walk-
ing in an African town and seeing three young African
children playing a game which was accompanied by handclapping. This sight, of course, is not an uncommon one in
our own country. What captured our attention was the
rhythmic pattern which these children were beating out

with their hands. Instead of the expected rhythmic pattern which one might hear in America, accompanying the chanting of "Ring Around the Rosy,"

the African children were clapping the following rhythm:

When pounding millet or maize, a woman will beat out a rhythm on the mortar with her pestle. A blacksmith blowing the bellows proceeds to play a tune on it. A girl, sitting idly, begins to tap with her fingers on a nearby basin. This strong emphasis on rhythm in African music does not mean there is the same kind of basic underlying beat as there is in Western music, particularly pop music. Actually, this steady beat, so strongly and loudly amplified by our hard rock bands today, is conspicuously absent from African music. The idea of a piece of music being in three-quarter time, as for example, "The Blue Danube" waltz, is quite un-African. In our music, we can clap our hands and beat out the basic rhythm of a waltz, a march, a popular tune, or even a Beethoven symphony because the accented beats occur with predictable regularity. But African hands, the most commonly used instrument to provide rhythmic background for singing, do not clap with this Western-style, hypnotic regularity. The important difference between the handclapping that you hear in Africa and that which you hear accompanying singing in America is that the African seems to be clapping in the "wrong" places at the "wrong" times, but that the "mistakes" occur with precision and are made with absolute perfection. In African music, unlike ours, there is not necessarily a connection between the regularly recurring accents of the melody and the handclapping. They seem to be going on independently and this is both frustrating as well as fascinating to the Westerner. How can people be such supreme masters of rhythm and so "off beat" at the same time?

A simple illustration of what might happen if you attempted to sing the familiar American folk song, "Here We Go 'Round the Mulberry Bush," accompanying it with African-style handclapping is:

Here we go 'round the mul-ber-ry bush, the

If the experience of trying to sing this song in African musical idiom proves to be too difficult, relax and do it as an American or European child would:

Here we go 'round the mul-ber-ry bush, the

Perhaps you can now begin to understand one of the fundamental differences between rhythm in traditional African music and rhythm in traditional Western music.

Another characteristic of African rhythm is called *cross-rhythm*. When the accents of a song follow shortly after the accents of an accompanying rhythm instrument or handclapping, cross-rhythm occurs. Try to imagine both parts, the song and the rhythmic accompaniment, having the identical underlying rhythmic pattern—⅜ time, for example:

Accompanying rhythm instrument:

Song or vocal part:

In our Western frame of reference, the lower part— the vocal part—would be called "syncopated"; that is, the

34

accents do not occur after each bar line in a regularly recurring and predictable way. In Western music there is an underlying basic rhythmic pattern. This consists of a series of beats with regularly recurring accents. A bar line is put directly in front of the most strongly accented note. In other words, when we look at a piece of Western music we know that the note immediately following a bar line is to be the most strongly accented one. When the beat immediately following the bar line is not accented, and when an accent occurs in an unpredictable way, the result is syncopation.

The African, however, doesn't think in terms of "bar lines" any more than he thinks in terms of "scales." As a result, syncopation in African music doesn't exist from the African's point of view. If the Westerner insists on using bar lines, then why not simply keep shifting the bar line as the accents keep changing! Syncopation can only occur in the Western context of a regularly recurring accent—that is, syncopation constitutes the process of rebelling against the regularly recurring accent. Can you imagine trying to march to an accompanying rhythm of

Left, right, left, right, left, right

without the accent always falling on the first beat? This would be syncopation. However, if we decided that it was not important for everyone to march in step with everyone's left foot coming down at the same time, then each person would adopt his own pattern of accents. For some it might be:

Left, right, left, right

and for others it would be:

Left, right, left, right

Each one establishes his own bar lines. Where there is no bar line to rebel against, there is no syncopation as we know it. The result is very African, very exciting and extremely frustrating for the person who tries to write the music down. The Dogon of Mali, who seem to have a passion for explaining everything, say that this characteristic of pitting one rhythmic pattern such as a waltz, against another such as a march, came to be because in order to achieve a state of perfection in anything, one must have a male and female principle uniting. The symbolism is genital: Triple time is male and double or quadruple is female. This idea is a common one; many West African tribes even regard some instruments as male or female. Even in a solo performance on a stringed instrument, the left hand might play in ¾ time while the right hand plays in ⁴⁄₄:

The rhythmic complexity of an African "choral symphony"—an expression used by Father A.M. Jones, England's distinguished authority on African music—can hardly be overstated. Each drum has its own rhythmic role; the singer's handclapping has yet another, and so have the rattles, the melody and the dancing. To quote Father Jones again, "From this there emerges a resultant rhythm which is different from each of the constituent rhythms. This is a sort of rhythmic harmony—a building up of rhythmic chords."

Lest anyone think that the result is some kind of musical anarchy, ("Every man for himself without any regard for others") let him be assured that such is not the case. There is usually one musician who beats out a short rhythmic phrase, usually on a gong or bell, that provides a common point of reference for all the other musicians. This short rhythmic phrase is called the *time-line* and is repeated in the same form over and over again throughout the entire performance. It acts as a yardstick by means of which each performer (from drummer to singer) can determine his rhythmic relationship to every other performer.

In a real sense, the time-line acts as a guide for the music and those who make it. The ability to follow the various rhythmic phrases and how they relate to the time-line is important, not only for the making of African music but for its appreciation as well. The African is taught from

AFRICAN ORCHESTRA, SIERRA LEONE; 2 DRUMS, 2 XYLOPHONES, 1 TAMBOURINE, 1 FLUTE

childhood to acquire this ability and to develop what has been described as the *metronome sense*. He can also articulate this time-line by moving his body in any one of a number of ways, such as the lurching of the shoulders, shaking of the head, stamping of the foot, etc. As a matter of fact, the various basic rhythmic patterns in African music can be reflected in the movements of different parts of the body. For example, while the arms move to one basic rhythmic pulsation, the legs will move to another and the shoulders to yet another.

Here is an example (from an African point of view) of a simple and uncomplicated song. The song is actually sung to the accompaniment of an *mbira* (African thumb piano). However, a guitar can be a satisfactory substitute. The guitar player would begin with the following four-bar phrase:

You will notice that there are two melodies, upper and lower, each with its own distinct rhythmic structure. The guitarist would then begin to sing the song as the four-bar phrase is repeated over and over again. It all sounds uncomplicated. It is, however, not a simple matter to play 6 against 4, and in addition, sing a melody against both. Here are the three melodies which play against one another (the upper and lower parts played by the guitar, plus the sung melody):

RWIYO RWEDANDE

(S. Rhodesia)

Sung Melody:

O-ye,   O-

Guitar or Mbira

ye,

O-ye,   yei-   ye,   O-

ye,   O-ye   O- ye-i   yei-

ye.

This is an example of an African melody sung and played, in which a simple rhythmic drama is acted out.

More and more now, it becomes apparent that one of the fundamental reasons why African music sounds so strange to our Western ears is that the rhythmic background used by the African for his song is vastly different from the rhythmic background Western musicians use. In the final analysis, in order to really begin to appreciate this prime difference, African music must become a personal experience. Ideally, you can pack your bags, leave a note for the milkman and go off to Africa where you can immediately join with Africans in singing their songs and dancing their dances. The alternative is to practice singing an African song, providing it with a rhythmic accompaniment in as authentic an African way as possible. It was in this spirit that a talented musician and master drummer from Ghana was asked to each some African songs to a group of students who knew nothing about African music and had never been to Africa. The musician, Alfred Ladzekpo, took this group for a couple of hours each day for five days and taught them to sing a few songs. One of the songs used comes from the Ewe people of Ghana and is called "*Ta Avɔ Na Legba*." It is performed in the following manner: A group of people form a circle. One of them acts as a cantor (leader) and starts the song. The rest sing the chorus. Then, in a spontaneous fashion, various members of the group take turns at being the cantor.

You can easily practice "*Ta Avɔ Na Legba*" using any percussion instrument such as the bell or gong. (Even a cooking pot, turned upside down, struck with a wooden spoon, can serve the purpose.)

42

TA AVƆ NA LEGBA

Taa-vɔ na leg-ba yi-ye!

Taa-vɔ na leg-ba yi-ye! Ta-ma-kloe ho-tsui-tɔ ne

Taa-vɔ na leg-ba leg-ba lea-vi ɔzi bea

vɔ la me-su yeo, yi-ye-he! *

It becomes noticeable in short order that the rhythm of the bell pattern and the accents of the vocal line do not, somehow, "match." They seem to lead independent lives and therein is the secret of both the strangeness and excitement of African music.

FORM IN
AFRICAN MUSIC

The basic elements of musical form are 1) *repetition*, 2) *variation* and 3) *contrast*. Repetition is essential because music is constantly in motion and the process of repetition is the means by which we become familiar with it. Music, unlike a painting, cannot stand still long enough for our ears to capture it in the same way that our eyes can capture a painting. Variation is necessary because unchanging repetition drives most people out of their minds. Contrast, too, reflects basic human needs—the overwhelming desire to stop what we are doing for an activity completely different— leave the city for a day in the country, soak in the sun after a long gray winter, and so on.

How has the African dealt with these basic elements of musical form? Before we answer this question, it must be stated as strongly as possible that form in music is determined by content. In other words, what a person has to say will affect the way he says it. How one puts together music— the form or shape it assumes—depends to a large degree on what the composer or the music maker is trying to say, the function which he wants the music to perform and the role which music plays in his society.

As we have already seen, there are many African melodies in which the music is regarded as a vehicle for the words. The poet and the composer are one and the same. With this kind of music, so closely bound to words, the form of an African song is obviously going to be derived partly from the text on which the melody is based or from which the melody springs. Happily, there is always room for improvisation and for the rearrangement of the order of verses, so that the actual form of a song grows out of a situation in which it is sung.

We have also seen that music plays an important role in the communal life of Africans. The songs and dances reflecting their traditional way of life promote and preserve a feeling of solidarity among the people of a given tribe.

Group singing, in which a leader (cantor) and people (chorus) alternate with each other performing a song, is one of the most important forms in African music. Usually there is one cantor, although two or three cantors are not uncommon. The simplest song form consists of a melody made up of two sections, (A and B), sung alternately by a cantor and a chorus, which may be repeated over and over again. The role of the cantor is creatively demanding. Not only does he decide what song is to be sung, but he is also the one who improvises and determines what variations are to be introduced and how long the song should last. This A—B form of music making is sometimes referred to as *call and response* singing and is most popular throughout Africa.

The participants follow and listen with intense interest to the leader's narrative. It can deal with an event from the life of a past chief, the history of the tribe, or typical events within the tribe or village community. Often the leader will improvise on current events.

You can hear the call and response pattern in many of the spirituals or gospel songs of the black American. "Go Down, Moses" and "Swing Low, Sweet Chariot" are two of many examples of this musical form. And, just as the main concern of African music had been to recite the history of the tribe, so, too, the slave in America discovered events in the Bible which paralleled his own situation. In "Go Down, Moses" he was singing about a man who had led his people out of slavery; Canaan, the Israelites' promised land, became a vision of freedom.

"Go Down, Moses"
(the leader sings): "When Israel was in Egypt's land,"
(the chorus replies): "Let my people go."
(the leader): "Oppressed so hard they could not stand,"
(the chorus): "Let my people go."

"Swing Low, Sweet Chariot"
(the leader sings) "I looked over Jordan and what did I see,"
(the chorus replies): "Coming for to carry me home,"
(the leader): "A band of angels coming after me,"
(the chorus): "Coming for to carry me home."

This kind of contrasting interplay of leader and chorus is also found in the relationship between the African master drummer and the secondary drums as well as the other instruments—a relationship which permits the leader to

46

improvise and then, together with the others, collaborate in unfolding a music drama.

In general, small forms are emphasized in much of African music. Pieces are repeated for as long as desired by the performers, the dancers or the actors, although variations may be found in each repetition and the instrumental accompaniment may be changed. Improvisation plays a more important part in African music than in Western music with the exception of jazz. Just as in jazz, where a solo performer will improvise against the supporting background of the other musicians in the band, so the leader in African music making is the one whose creative imagination plays with the words and music of a particular song against the stable background provided by the chorus.

On the whole, rhythm and its development is the focal point of attention in African music rather than the melody or theme and its development, as in the case of Western music. And just as one of the means by which we evaluate composers of traditional Western music is by the extent of their inventiveness in developing simple thematic material, (look at what Beethoven did with four simple notes in his Fifth Symphony), an African musician is judged outstanding on the basis of his ability to develop the rhythmic patterns.

In African vocal music, it is the text which is the center of interest rather than the melody. It should always be remembered that African music is designed primarily for *use*, and the essential fact remains that there is a definite correlation between the functional role that music plays in African society and the way that Africans organize the materials of music.

Generally speaking, in the music of Western civilization it has been the melody which has challenged the creative capacities of the composer. As a matter of fact, one of the means by which Westerners judge the "goodness" or "greatness" or "beauty" of a piece of music is the way a composer takes a simple melody or a part of a melody and develops it, as in a symphony, or turns it upside down and inside out, as in a fugue. The element of melodic *variation* receives a great deal of attention in Western music, more so than in African music. African music is a mixture of *variation* and *repetition*. However, the repetitive element receives greater stress than the variation element. In a typical performance, most of the musicians sing or play the same short melodies and rhythmic patterns over and over again, while the leader provides the variation. Much of the distinction of African music lies in this subtle interplay between *repetition* and *variation*, as well as in the dramatic and exciting *contrasts* of different basic rhythms.

Art is not separated from function in African society and artistry is not an end in itself. Artistic and social values operate at one and the same time. African musicians would certainly support the late British art historian, Sir Herbert Read, who once described beauty in the arts as "suitability for purpose"—a dynamic and functional interpretation of the philosophy of beauty.

It is easy to understand if we think of how we evaluate a thing as ordinary as a pencil. The dynamic and functional approach would be to ask: "Does it work?" "Does it write effectively?" The aesthetic view would be to ask, "Is it beautiful?" From the point of view of the African musician or Sir Herbert Read, the beauty of the pencil is determined

48

by the effectiveness with which it performs the function it was designed to perform. And so, if the sound of African music, its form and style, are different from the sounds of Western music, it must be remembered that in some fundamental respects, music has a different meaning in the two parts of the world.

* RATTLE

49

AFRICAN MUSICAL INSTRUMENTS

Where music is found to be woven into the very fabric of people's lives, it is likely that the people will be personally involved both in the process of making the instruments as well as the music itself. And, just as the quality of craftsmanship in music making is not shared equally by all tribes or the individuals in them, so, too, are there significant differences in the art of making instruments and the kind of instruments made among both individuals and groups.

Environment has affected the kinds of instruments produced in various parts of Africa. If there were no trees or reeds from which to make musical instruments, the people turned to singing only. This is especially noticeable in the southern tip of Africa where only one percent of the entire country was covered by natural woods. Few drums are to be found in South Africa; their music is almost exclusively vocal with simple accompaniments such as handclapping and stamping.

Among the earliest recorded observations about African music were those made and written down by the mid-sixteenth-century Portuguese explorers and missionaries. Travelling in Central and Southern Africa, they remarked on the instruments which accompanied the chiefs upon their journeys, the presence of numerous musicians in the royal households, and the continual singing and dancing in which everyone participated.

The three kinds of musical instruments most frequently mentioned were the *drum*, the *xylophone* and the *mbira*, the last being a peculiarly African instrument consisting of a number of short metal reeds and which has no European equivalent. (In later times, the mbira was misnamed the "kaffir piano." A *Kaffir* is a member of one of the Bantu tribes of South Africa.)

THE DRUM

The most widely used instrument in Africa is the *drum*. Africans drum when they are happy and they drum when they are sad. On important state occasions such as the welcoming of a visiting dignitary from a foreign land, the drum can be the most important musical instrument played, with the drummer's status, accordingly, impressively high. An African child will drum on almost anything he can put his hands and fingers on. He will drum on tables, chairs, boxes, packing cases and kerosene tins. To say that Africans are fond of drumming is an understatement. It's more accurate to say the only time he doesn't drum is when he is asleep!

51

Why do Africans find drumming so exciting? For part of the answer we have to look at the role that drums play in an African's life, and remember that what a drummer plays has a meaning. In Africa, drums *say* something and an African drums for a *purpose*. Take the *talking* drums of the Ashanti people of Ghana, for example. The drummer actually talks with the *atumpan* drum, and similar stories can be told of drums found in other parts of Africa. The talking drums of Africa are essentially language drums.

You will remember that most African languages are tonal languages. A higher-pitched drum corresponds to the high-pitched syllable and a lower-pitched drum to the low-pitched syllable. This enables the drummer to send messages. For instance, a European coming into the forest would be described as "A man from the outside world coming to the forest"; a native would be described as "returning home." Talking drums can be heard as far away as six or seven miles, and from that point the message can be relayed another six or seven miles, and so on.

When the African was brought to the United States as a slave, he brought with him his music and dance, his history and his religion; he brought with him his memories and his way of life. This cultural heritage was systematically and deliberately destroyed. Religious practices, along with the music and dance, the drums and the rattles and the bells, all of which were an integral part of African religion and the African way of life, were banned in many parts of America. They were forbidden because of a fear of "subversive activities." There were, after all, some one hundred and thirty major slave revolts which occurred between 1663 and 1865. Legislation was enacted, making it unlawful for the African to play his drums, and for the slaves

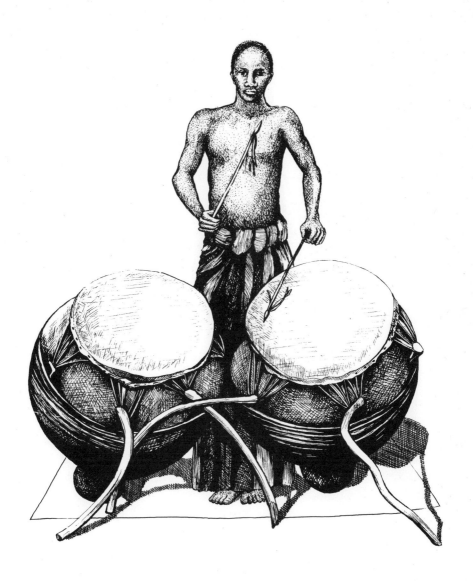

*ATUMPAN DRUMS

FONTOMFROM DRUMS — TALL ASHANTI TALKING
DRUMS, USED IN FONTOMFROM ORCHESTRA FOR
ROYAL OCCASIONS

to gather even for the purpose of dancing. In 1817, for
example, the Municipal Council of New Orleans issued an
ordinance forbidding slave gatherings for the purpose of
dancing except on Sundays and only in places designated by
the Mayor. Congo Square (today known as Beauregard
Square) was established as the place for such dances, but
only under police supervision.

Undoubtedly, such modern inventions in the twentieth
century as the telephone and other communication sys-
tems have taken the place of the drums as means of communication between Africans. However, up until a relatively
short time ago, the talking drums of Africa were an effec-

tive way for Africans to communicate with each other. A highly skilled drummer or a master drummer can perform messages on the drums because he is able to play the variety of rhythms which are part of the vocabulary of any language, as well as the rising and falling pitch levels of the African tonal languages.

It takes years of practice and experience to become a *master drummer* and, once having achieved the status, the master drummer is publicly recognized as an outstanding artist. The fact is that a good African master drummer is a distinguished musician, judged by any standards, African or Western. The African talking drums are capable of producing a wide range of tones which all fall within the range of the adult male's speaking voice. But let us take a look at how a drum actually talks.

To begin with, a good drummer can produce different tones by the way he plays the drum. It can be played with the palms of the hand, the fingers, a stick or any combination of these. Or, a drummer can produce a wide range of tones of different pitches with the *donno* drum in West Africa. It is commonly referred to as the *hourglass* drum because of its shape. The hourglass is a double-headed drum which is held in the left armpit. The left arm squeezes the strings which hold the drum heads together, thereby tightening and loosening the drum heads and raising and lowering the pitch.

When the drumming is associated with dancing, singing or some kind of drama, the African generally uses a full ensemble of drums, or a drum orchestra. Often rattles and bells are added. When an African wishes to "speak," however, he uses only one drum or a pair of drums. When a pair of drums is used—for example, the atumpan drums—

DONNO DRUM — HOURGLASS SQUEEZE DRUM

one of them speaks with a low voice (it is called a male drum), and the other with a high voice (this is the female drum).

African drums talk by imitating the way African people talk. First, they imitate the rhythm of the words and phrases which make up the sentences of African languages. This is why African children are taught to play drums by means of words and sentences. You can easily demonstrate for yourself how this works by handclapping the rhythm of the words of a familiar poem or song, syllable by syllable. If the rhythm is clearly articulated, it will make the poem or song recognizable to your listener.

Secondly, the African drummer imitates the various tones or pitch level—the high, the low and those inbetween—of the language. For example, in the language of Twi (pronounced "chwee") the question, *Wo din de sen* means "What is your name?" There are four syllables in this sentence; the first is a low tone, the second high, the third low and the fourth high. And so, the drummer will play his male and female drums as follows:

1	2	3	4
male	female	male	female
Wo	din	de	sen

(What is your name?)

You can see how important it is to learn how to listen to the talking drums, as well as play them.

Sometimes other instruments are added to the drums. Basically, however, a traditional African orchestra can consist of an ensemble of drums—drums of every size and shape —just as the basic ingredient of the traditional Western orchestra is an ensemble of strings. An African drum orchestra can produce a variety of different tonal qualities as well as pitch levels. Some of the drums have a high pitch, others have a low pitch, and others are inbetween. Some drums have a hard piercing tone, others have a clear ringing tone, and others sound heavy or dull.

DRUM, SOUTHERN NIGERIA

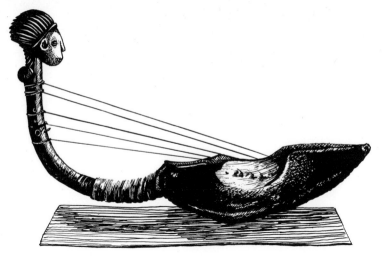

AFRICAN HARP — COVERED WOOD, OF THE
AZANDA PEOPLE IN NORTHEAST CONGO

In addition, there are orchestras which correspond to our
Western chamber music ensembles. Some of them concen-
trate on stringed instruments, others on brass and woodwinds. In Africa, it is possible to have an orchestra of four
horns plus rhythm; three flutes plus rhythm or three xylophones plus rhythm.

There is one example of an African instrument ensemble
where the drums are completely absent. This is a string
orchestra. In its traditional setting in Nigeria, the string ensemble is a trio, consisting of a string player, a singer chanting in monotone and a third musician supplying rhythmic
accompaniment on a large gourd known as a calabash.

In the musical ensembles which consist primarily of
wind or string instruments, the emphasis is on melodic improvisation rather than rhythmic improvisation.

And so now another myth about Africa can be laid to
rest—the assumption that African musical instruments consist only of drums. Actually, most of the varieties of musical instruments known to man are to be found in Africa.

59

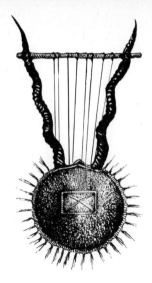

KISSAR LYRE, CENTRAL AFRICA; GOURD BODY DECO-
RATED WITH BRISTLES AND UPRIGHTS OF ANTELOPE
HORN

They include examples of the four categories of instruments which have been set up by musicologists and anthro-
pologists:

1) *Idiophones*—Instruments whose entire bodies vibrate,
such as rattles, bells, xylophones, hand
pianos, etc.
2) *Membranophones*—Instruments with vibrating mem-
branes or parchment skins, such
as drums.
3) *Aerophones*—Instruments which enclose a body of
vibrating air, such as flutes and trumpets.
4) *Chordophones*—Instruments with vibrating strings,
such as fiddles, lutes, zithers, etc.

In Western music, we classify musical instruments as
percussion (membranophones and idiophones); *strings*
(chordophones); and *woodwinds* and *brass* (aerophones).

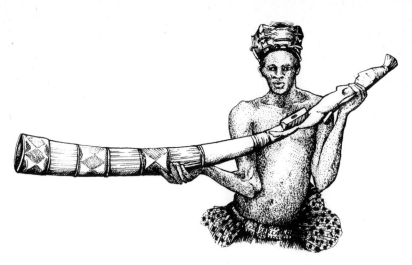

CARVED IVORY TRUMPET, MANGBETU TRIBE OF
CENTRAL AFRICA

One instrument has strangely escaped classification by
the scholars in spite of the fact that it may very well be an
even more widely used percussion instrument than the
drum. It is the human body. Not merely torso, not only
limbs, but the *body* has been used as a percussion instrument in Africa more effectively than probably anywhere
else in the world. An amusing challenge is to think of the
different ways in which you can turn yourself into a
"percussion" instrument: you might try clapping your
hands, stamping your feet, clacking your tongue, slapping
your chest or thigh. You might even try tapping your
open mouth while singing and listening for the changes
in the resonance of your voice. Try singing a song and
improvising several different patterns of rhythmic accompaniment, using your own body exclusively. The next step
is to share the experience: Gather your friends some evening
and divide them into handclappers, knee slappers, foot
stampers, finger clickers, tongue clackers, or any other
"body musician," each one playing a different rhythm while

everyone sings a familiar song. Imagine the distinction of establishing the first "Body Percussion Ensemble" in your neighborhood!

THE XYLOPHONE

Another instrument commonly found in many parts of Africa is the *xylophone*, several types of which are indigenous to West, Central, East and Southeast Africa. Differences exist in the musical functions they perform, and the type of musical ensemble in which they participate. Xylophones are played alone; they are played along with drums; they are played as an accompaniment to singing and dancing; they are played in orchestras of xylophones.

There are xylophones which can play only several different notes and there are xylophones which can play about thirty different notes. There may be one, two, three or as many as six performers on a single xylophone, and a solo musician may use only one or as many as four beaters or mallets in performance. African xylophones are constructed in a variety of ways, and from a variety of materials. Some instruments, known as *log xylophones*, consist of a set of wooden keys laid across banana trunks. Banana trunks make excellent cushions for the keys to rest on and enable the keys to vibrate freely. In addition, banana trunks, because they are hollow inside, are excellent resonators. Sometimes, wooden keys are simply laid across the performer's legs, sometimes they are laid across two trees that have been cut down. In West Africa, a commonly found xylophone consists of wooden keys, supported on a wooden frame, with each key having its own gourd or calabash resonator hanging beneath.

There is strong evidence that the xylophone may also have originated in Africa. Reportedly, it was in use in Mali in the thirteenth century and this predates its first appearance in Europe by a couple of hundred years. It is almost certain that an African xylophone was brought to the Americas on the first slave ships which sailed from Mozambique to South America. Have you heard of the *marimba?* It is one of the most popular instruments in Latin America and has been incorporated into the music of the United States and Europe. *Marimba* is an African (Bantu) word for the wooden xylophone with resonators found along the East Africa coast. That makes the African xylophone the ancestor of our marimba.

XYLOPHONE WITH GOURD RESONATORS

THE MBIRA

Second only to the drum as the most popular folk instrument in Africa is the *mbira*. It is a small instrument with a number of metal reeds of varying length which are attached to a sounding board or box and which you pluck with your thumbs. The pitch is determined by the length of the metal reed and the number of reeds will vary, anywhere from seven to eight, to fifteen or more. The mbira, which has over one hundred different African names, originated in Africa. It is sometimes referred to as a "thumb piano" or "hand piano." An intimate instrument, the mbira is ideally appropriate to personal music making. It produces a soft and gentle sound and is also especially suited for fast playing. The first non-Africans to "discover" the mbira were Portuguese explorers in the 16th century. Father Dos Santos, a Portuguese priest and missionary, wrote the following about the mbira in 1586:

> *It is all made of irons about a palm in length, tempered in the fire so that each has a different sound . . . They strike the keys as lightly as a good player strikes those of the harpsichord. Thus the iron rods being shaken, and the blows resounding above the hollow of the bowl . . . they produce altogether a sweet and gentle harmony of accordant sounds . . . It is very soft and makes but little noise.*

Interestingly enough, the mbira, *invented by Africans,* has a delicate and sensitive tonal quality, and is completely different from the "big" sound we have been brought up to expect from African instruments. Come to think of it, we don't remember seeing a single mbira in any of the Tarzan pictures.

The few instruments we described are a mere sampling of the many the African uses as tools to fashion his music. It is not unreasonable to conclude that in the hands of an African just about anything can be, and is, used as a musical instrument. In a society where the making of music is part of the very process of living, this should offer no surprise; for, in reality, the sounds of African music are the sounds of Africans at work and at play.

MBIRA — THUMB PIANO, WITH GOURD RESONATOR

THE MUSIC OF CONTEMPORARY AFRICA

We began this book about African music by saying that the music is strange to our Western ears. Then we proceeded to describe those characteristics of African music which make it sound so different from the music of Western civilization—the music with which we have been raised. But, in the words of Bob Dylan, "The times, they are a-changin'."

Today, when you visit the larger towns and cities in Africa, particularly the record stalls and dance halls where young people gather, the sounds of music have a "back home" familiarity. Young Africans are caught up with the same soul music that fascinates the young generation of Americans. The names Ray Charles, Lou Rawls and B. B. King are as recognizable as the Coca-Cola label, and these performers are as popular in modern-day Ghana, for instance, as they are in America.

However, modern Africa has done more than merely import American soul music. It has developed its own contemporary version of pop—the irresistible African "High-life." According to A.M. Jones, it became the craze in the mid-forties in Northern Rhodesia where it was first called "Makwaya" (MA-choir). In Uganda they call it "Cheta"; in South Africa it is called "Township Jazz"; and in West Africa it is "Highlife." This new popular music which is growing throughout modern Africa, and to which we shall refer as Highlife, is essentially a synthesis of Western and African music. While its resemblance to our jazz of the 1940's is noticeable, even under its African clothing, there is no mistaking its unquestionable African style.

Highlife is basically vocal music. Even when played by instruments, there will always be a vocal interlude. It is sung in the various African languages, although occasionally one can find Highlife in English.

Highlife songs, in company with the Blues and Calypso, (which are African influenced) deal in an unescapist way with all kinds of subjects close to the African man in the street: the eternal quality of love; women, and the inexhaustible variations on that venerable and treasured theme; work, and the hardships from the lack of it; education, and the frustrations from the lack of it; the sorrow of death; people who are remarkable for any of the reasons in the spectrum of human behavior—wisdom, strength, greed, skill; events that are memorable for their impact on the history of a country or a single tribal group. Highlife songs recognize all the trials and joy of man. They stem from earlier African attitudes to music and carry on the strong tradition of social comment and satire. It is also in Highlife that the African will give expression to his criticism of his political leaders and praise his heroes.

This new music is a product of the urbanization of African society since World War II. Young Africans, leaving their villages in the country and moving to the larger towns and cities, saw Europeans dancing in nightclubs and ball-rooms to the latest American song hits. It was not long be-fore Africans learned to drink Coca-Cola and sing the latest American song hits, too.

Not surprisingly, the avalanche of popularity of the guitar swept into Africa and today, just as in America and Europe, young Africans are teaching themselves to play. For many of the younger generation, the guitar is replacing the mbira as the instrument played for personal pleasure. In recent years Dr. Hugh Tracey, Director of the International So-ciety of African Music, introduced the thumb piano to Americans. Sold under the name, "Kalimba," it is light-weight, portable and easy to play and beginning to enjoy a wide and growing popularity. What a nice touch of irony it would be to see the thumb piano replace the guitar as America's favorite amateur instrument—a beautiful ex-ample of a non-governmental-supported cultural exchange program.

At first, African musicians copied the essentially bland and unexciting Western dance music which Europeans en-joyed. However, when more and more Africans began to patronize these ballrooms, dance halls and nightclubs, a demand was created for a more varied and exciting kind of dance music. Highlife represents a blending of African tra-ditional forms and Western music.

During the last decade, as African countries have achieved independence, Highlife has become increasingly and con-sciously African in style and content, evolving into a com-pletely original form. At the same time, *we* are becoming more aware of the African influences on our music, the most outstanding of which is jazz.

Jazz, ranking high in the musical achievements of the twentieth century, would simply not exist without Africa. It is the product of the black African's experiences in America. During the eighteenth and nineteenth centuries, millions of Africans were brought to the Americas to work as slaves —to Brazil, the West Indies and—by far the largest proportion—to the United States.

The slaves in America, many of whom had been converted to Christianity, were taught to sing Protestant hymns. When the African sang the Christian hymns of his masters, he often imposed his own musical traditions by flattening the third and seventh notes of the scale because he was unable to cope with our scales.

Another African musical characteristic which was incorporated into the spirituals or gospel songs (the African slaves' version of the Protestant hymn) is the call and response pattern used in the congregational singing in the American black man's church. Both of these characteristics are African, and they have survived in jazz from the earliest times to the present day.

We can also see the effect that the functional role which African music played in African society had on the spirituals of the African slave in America. These spirituals reflected not only religious faith, exemplified in such famous songs as "Go Tell It On The Mountain" and "Didn't My Lord Deliver Daniel," they also echoed the protest of an oppressed people, expressing their despair and desolation in "Sometimes I Feel Like A Motherless Child."

After the Civil War and the emancipation of the slaves, spirituals changed from protest songs to blues. The blues was an expression of the new problems and hardships of the Afro-American as a "free" man. As a musical form, the blues has run like a spine throughout the entire history of jazz.

The influences of African music have been widespread, in some cases following a circuitous route—from Africa to the Americas and back to Africa again. Most modern African dance bands, for example, use the same instruments that ours do—guitar, string bass, conga drum, bongo drum, saxophone, trumpet and trombone. Yet the concept of a rhythm section consisting of stringed instruments with drums laying down a rhythmic base for singing is *African in origin*. Both Latin-American and jazz rhythm sections are developments of the mixed groups of lutes, mbiras and drums heard all over West Africa. It's only fair and just, after all, that Highlife makes use of Latin-American rhythms. These rhythms went to the Americas via the slave ships. They have been renovated, overhauled and returned home.

The similarities and differences between American and African pop music seem equally divided. But one of the most critical disparities is that theirs is built on African conceptions of rhythm and is, therefore, far more rhythmically interesting than ours with its basic underlying relentlessly and regularly recurring accented beat.

As fundamentally un-African as the roots of Highlife are, it is a combination of the twentieth century white European and American dance music and African musical characteristics and practices. An example of the "un-African" aspect of Highlife is that whereas the genuine village dance is a communal enterprise in which everyone takes part, and there are no professional performers, the new pop music demands that the majority of people should be spectators and listeners rather than participants.

70

Contrastingly, the tribal upbringing of the African which has taught him to be a participant rather than a listener has had its effect on the development of contemporary African pop music. By American standards many of the African dance bands seem to be rather crude. They do not perform with the same degree of polish and precision to which we are accustomed.

The typical African musician is self-taught, working at a trade with music as an avocation (a strong resemblance to the early self-taught American jazz musicians). Most of the Highlife bands, continuing in the tradition of the praise bands, are cooperatives. All the members equally divide the money received as payment for their musical services. There are relatively few professional bands—most of the musicians have day jobs. African dance band musicians do not, therefore, have the desire or the needed time to improve their skills in Western music. Undoubtedly, one reason for this state of affairs is to be found in the African audience. The African does not passively listen to a live or recorded performance of a dance band. His entire heritage impels him to participate. He moves his body. He sings the lyrics. He becomes *involved* with the performance. Consequently, he reacts with somewhat less than overwhelming approval or appreciation to either the slickest performance of an American-type dance band, because he finds the music rhythmically uninteresting, or to the dazzling pyrotechnics or the unorthodox sounds produced by some of our contemporary avant-garde jazz musicians because they deny him the opportunity to either move his body or sing the words.

In the absence of a tradition of music listening, therefore, Africans tend to judge band performance solely on their reaction to the rhythm or the words. Highlife and soul

MODERN AFRICAN PLAYING A NOTCHED FLUTE

music—music that is either rhythmically or textually interesting—is popular, while the waltz, fox-trot, and other such types of dancing are tolerated, and appreciated by only a minority.

However African music is made, by any of the enormous variety of plucked, beaten, strummed or shaken instruments, and wherever it is made, village or city, home or cabaret, it is a vital expression of an indomitable people.

For all its strangeness to the Western ear, African music is no exotic museum piece, suitable only for study by inquisitive musicologists. Whether reflective of the strong African tradition of social comment or performing its function in perpetuating a people's moral code and way of life, African music is as vital as its people who are now engaged in carving out independent futures. No longer can it be set on a shelf marked "to be studied as a curiosity—not to be taken seriously."

Accepted on its own terms, African music is not inferior. It is simply different. The traditional African praise song is as culturally legitimate as a song by Schubert. A people's music is its mirror. We are fortunate to live in a time when we can hear Africa's music, and begin to know Africa's people.

BIBLIOGRAPHY

AND

DISCOGRAPHY

Books

BOHANNON, Paul, *Africa and Africans*, Garden City, N. Y.: Doubleday & Co., 1964

BRANDEL, Rose, *The Music of Central Africa*, The Hague, Netherlands: Martinus Nijhoft, 1961

DIETZ, Betty Warner and OLATUNJI, Michael Babatunde, *Musical Instruments of Africa*, New York: John Day, 1965.

HOWARD, Joseph, *Drums in the Americas*, New York: Oak Publications, 1967

HUGHES, Langston, *The First Book of Africa*, New York: Franklin Watts, 1965

JONES, A. M., *Studies In African Music*, London: Oxford University Press, 1959. 2 vols.

KYAGAMBIDDWA, Joseph, *African Music From the Source of the Nile*, New York: Frederick A. Praeger, 1955

LYSTAD, Robert, Ed., *The African World*, New York: Frederick A. Praeger, 1965

MERRIAM, Alan P., *A Prologue to the Study of the African Arts*, Yellow Springs: Antioch Press, 1962

NKETIA, J. H. Kwabena, *African Music in Ghana*, Evanston, Illinois: Northwestern University Press, 1963

NKETIA, J. H. Kwabena, *Folk Songs of Ghana*, Legon, Ghana: University of Ghana, 1963

POWNE, Michael, *Ethiopian Music: An Introduction*, London: Oxford University Press, 1966

SUTHERLAND, Efua, *Playtime in Africa*, New York: Athenum, 1962

WEMEN, Henry, *African Music and the Church in Africa*, Uppsala, Sweden: Svenska Institutet for Missions forskning, 1960

In addition, the periodical, *African Arts*, a quarterly devoted to the graphic, plastic, performing and literary arts of Africa, is available from the African Studies Center, University of California, Los Angeles, California 90024.

Records

African Music (Folkways)
Songs From Kenya (Folkways)

Africa South of the Sahara (Folkways) 2 records
New Sounds From A New Nation—Ghana (Tempo)
New Sounds From A New Nation—Guinea (Tempo) 6
  records
This Land is Mine: South African Freedom Songs (Folk-
  ways)
African Music From the French Colonies (Columbia)
Music of the Cameroons (Folkways)
Drums of the Yoruba of Nigeria (Folkways)
Music of Equatorial Africa (Folkways)
Music of the Mende of Sierra Leone (Folkways)
Missa Luba (Phillips)
Music of Mali (Folkways)
Folk Music of Liberia (Folkways)
Wolof Music of Senegal & Gambia (Folkways)
Music of Chad (Folkways)
Music of the Falashas (Folkways)
Folk Music of Ethiopa (Folkways)
Music of the Ituri Forest People (Folkways)
Songs of the Congo (Epic)
Folk Songs of Africa (Bowmer) Record and book and
  2 color filmstrips
The Baoule of the Ivory Coast (Folkways)
Folk Music of the Western Congo (Folkways)
Olantunji—Flaming Drums (Columbia)
Olantunji Zungo (Columbia)
The Voices and Drums of Africa (Monitor)
Tuareg Music of the Southern Sahara (Folkways)
Music Malawi—1962 (Operation Crossroads Africa)

African Drums (Folkways)
Bantu Choral Folk Songs (Folkways)
Folk Music of Africa (African-American Institute)
Atumpan—The Talking Drums (U.C.L.A. Institute of Ethnomusicology)
The Voice of Africa—Miriam Makeba (R.C.A. Victor)
Songs from Africa—Belafonte & Makeba (Victor)
The World of Miriam Makeba (Victor)
Makeba Sings (Victor)
Miriam Makeba (Victor)
African Rhythms—Guy Warren (Decca)

The following records are part of *The Music of Africa Series.* They are authentic folk music recordings made in Central and Southern Africa and produced by and available from the

> International Library of African Music
> P. O. Box 138
> Roodepoort, Transvaal
> South Africa

African Dances of the Witwatersrand Gold Mines—Parts 1 & 2 (2 records)
African Music Society's Awards (3 records)
Songs from the Roadside: South Africa
Songs from the Roadside: Rhodesia
Music of the Northern Congo: Sudan

Music of the Northern Congo: Bantu
Music of Uganda
Music of Tanzania
Music of Rhodesia
Musical Instruments: Strings (harps, lyres, lutes and musical bows)
Musical Instruments: Mbira
Musical Instruments: Drums
Musical Instruments: Flutes & Horns
Musical Instruments: Xylophones
Musical Instruments: Guitars

Each record is approximately $6, delivered.

The Kalimba

Of all the many African instruments with which one can learn to produce the sounds of African music, only one is readily available.

If the excitement of actually *making* African music entices you, you can obtain the *Kalimba,* a new musical instrument with an old history—the latest member and direct descendant of the African family of instruments called *mbira.* It is inexpensive and a great deal of fun. For further information write to:

International Library of African Music
P. O. Box 138
Roodepoort, Transvaal
South Africa

APPENDIX

Notched flutes

These whistles frequently are found in Northern Ghana. Their shrill sound penetrates through a large ensemble of drums and viols. They frequently are heard at festival time. Because they are fragile, they are wrapped and put away when not in use.

Hand rattle

The hand rattle or gourd rattle is one of the most common instruments played in Africa. It may have internal or external strikers and is played by both male and female. The strikers may be of a variety of materials, such as pebbles, beads, or even the backbone of a python. Frequently the gourd rattle is used as an especially sacred instrument.

Fontomfrom Ensemble

Because this picture of a fontomfrom ensemble was taken in a chief's courtyard, the men's chests are bared (one must always bare his chest before the chief). The two small boys in front of the bomma drums are holding the pair, although sometimes one sees the drums being rested on a wooden stand. The drums are always covered for state occasion.

Musical bow

The musical bow is yet another example of how the African uses materials of his environment to make musical instruments. In playing, the musician holds the lower end of the bow firmly by the 2nd, 3rd and 4th fingers of the left hand. This leaves the 1st finger and thumb free to hold the stick which is pressed from time to time against a certain place on the string. In his right hand the player holds a small stick or reed with which he strikes the bow string with a staccato action. The bow is held so that it vibrates between the open lips but does not touch them.

Gondje

This type of gondje is from the Frafra who live in the vicinity of Bolgatanga in Northern Ghana. It came from the Hausa of Northern Nigeria and is found throughout West Africa. This Frafra gondje is more fragile and crude than the one which comes from the Dagamba (Tomak and Yendi area). One frequently sees the Frafra gondje being played for workers in the field who are slashing the grass with cutlasses.

Kalungu

This Hausan instrument from Northern Nigeria is plucked with the fingers. It is usually played by professional musicians.

Rattle

This notched stick is found all over Africa, and is used by both women's and men's groups.

Atumpan Drums

This is one of the talking drums in Ghana. It is from the Ashanti people and always comes as a pair, one male and one female. The drum set has been adopted by other groups in Ghana, but it is interesting that it "talks" in Ashanti; that is, the Ashanti tonal rhythms are played and interpreted in Ashanti. The set is included in the fontomfrom drum ensemble. The Atumpan is always found at the fetish shrine and at the chief's courtyard. During wartime, a chief dreaded most having his drums captured.

Ta avɔ na legba

Clothe the idol: Well done!
The worthy chief Tamakloe should clothe the idol.
The idol tearfully complains of insufficient clothing.

INDEX

85